PENGUINS
The Birds With Flippers

Penguins are the only birds in the world that have flippers instead of wings. And they are the only birds that stand and walk upright, like people.

In this book, Elizabeth Austin tells of the fascinating and amusing world of the penguins. She tells about each of the 15 different kinds of penguins and where they live, from Antarctica to the Equator. She tells about their unusual ways of courting and of caring for the young. And she describes many of the voyages of the early Antarctic explorers, in which men met penguins for the first time.

PENGUINS

The Birds
With Flippers

by ELIZABETH S. AUSTIN

Illustrated with photographs

 Random House · New York

For helpful suggestions in the preparation of this book, the author and the publisher are grateful to William J. L. Sladen, M.B.E., M.D., D. Phil., of Johns Hopkins University.

Photograph Credits: American Museum of Natural History, 27; Annan, 38 top right; Arthur Ambler (National Audubon Society), 73 left; Alfred Bailey (National Audubon Society), 69; J. Bechervaise (ANARE), 21 bottom; Bettmann Archive, 10; Birnback, 46; British Museum, 16; G. J. Broekhuysen, 75; John Brownlie (Photo Researchers Ltd.), 66; S. Csordas (ANARE), 60; Philip Gendreau (National Audubon Society), 12; Bell Howarth Ltd. (Black Star), 70; Russ Kinne (Photo Researchers), vi, 32; V. Koshevoi (Sovfoto), 42; Norman Laird (Pix), 56-57; P. G. Law (ANARE), 30; Fred Lewis (National Audubon Society), 62; William Maher, 43; K. Martin (ANARE), front endpapers; V. Martynov (Sovfoto), ii; Monkmeyer, 24; National Science Foundation, 48; New York Zoological Society, 17, 72 right; Pictorial Parade, 47, 53; Roy Pinney (Photo Library), 21 top; Pix, 38 bottom; H. G. Ponting (Bettmann Archive), 45; T. J. Regina (Photo Researchers), 34; Robert Reinhold (New York *Times*), back endpapers; San Diego Zoo, 50; Flip Schulke (Black Star), 73 right; Shostal, cover; Philip Smith (National Audubon Society), 5; M. F. Soper (National Audubon Society), 67; Wolf Suschitzky, 19, 22, 72 left; UPI, 2, 38 top left; A. Vrana (ANARE), 41; Ylla (Rapho Guillumette), 7.

Cover: Bob O'Reilly from Shostal Associates, Inc.

The chapter-opening motif is from a photograph by Russ Kinne (Photo Researchers).

The map on page 78 is by Ted Burwell.

Map information courtesy of James Fisher and Roger Tory Peterson from *The World of Birds* (Doubleday). Adapted by permission of Aldus Books Ltd.

Designed by Jackie Corner Mabli.

CONTENTS

PENGUINS
The Birds With Flippers

MEET
the
PENGUINS

Penguins are the only birds in the world that have flippers instead of wings. They are also the only birds that stand and walk about upright. With head and body erect, they look much like people. They stroll about in groups, their eyes forward, chests out, and flippers hanging where arms do on men. Their appearance is often compared to that of men in dark evening clothes and gleaming white shirts. Like all well-bred gentlemen, they bow and cackle to any strangers they meet, as well as to each other.

Probably the first Europeans to see a penguin were a Portuguese explorer, Bartholomew Dias, and

3

his crew. In the year 1488, before Columbus discovered America and when people still believed the world was flat, Dias discovered the Cape of Good Hope at the southern tip of Africa. He must have also discovered the Jackass Penguins, so plentiful there that no one could miss them. The explorers left no record of the meeting, but undoubtedly the penguins stared at the strangers, as they did at the many adventurous ships that followed.

It was not until 1740, more than 250 years later, that a British sailor brought a young Jackass Penguin back to England. It was described and painted by George Edwards, an artist-naturalist, in his book of natural history published in London. Between 1740 and 1871 explorers discovered 15 kinds, or *species,* of penguins, all found south of the equator.

Most pictures we see of penguins show them against a background of ice and snow. Actually only four species live in cold Antarctica. The other 11 species of penguins live off the coasts of subantarctic islands, South America, Africa, Australia, and New Zealand. One, the Galapagos Penguin, lives on the Galapagos Islands near the equator. Many penguins breed on ocean islands farther south. Wherever they live, cold currents that flow northward from Antarctica are important to them. The

4

cold currents carry the tiny shrimp called krill and the squid and fish that all penguins eat. Penguins only eat when they are in the water. They fast while on land.

On land penguins get around by walking, running, hopping, or jumping. When they are in a hurry many throw themselves down in a "belly whopper" and push themselves over the ice with their flippers. In the sea, penguins can row on the surface using their flippers as oars. They also dive and swim deep underwater. To breathe, they leap out of the water as porpoises do. Penguins stay at sea for months at a time. They are more at home in the water than any other birds. They even drink the salt sea water.

An Emperor Penguin doing a "belly whopper" on the ice.

All the birds in the world today, about 8,650 species, had flying ancestors. Yet a few of our modern birds no longer fly. Penguins are among these 47 living species that stopped flying. Very few flightless birds can escape enemies and survive. In the last 200 years, at least 30 species of flightless birds have become extinct. Penguins survive because they can escape enemies by swimming and diving.

Penguins first appeared on earth about 55 million years ago. Fossils of their prehistoric ancestors have been found in many of the places where penguins live today, and these prehistoric birds were very much like the modern ones—flightless water birds that walked erect. They were about the same size as penguins today, from 16 to 48 inches tall, except for one giant in New Zealand. This bird stood a full 5 feet and may have weighed over 100 pounds.

Flight is the main reason for the development of feathers, and penguins have feathers. Long ago penguin ancestors were probably flying sea birds similar to diving petrels. They gradually lost the flight feathers that make it possible for birds to be airborne. They found all they needed to sustain life without flying.

Most birds grow their feathers in patterns called "feather tracts," with patches of bare skin in be-

6

Feathers cover almost all of a penguin's body. Notice the tiny ones on the edge of the flippers.

tween. The feathers overlap the bare skin patches and cover them. A penguin grows feathers all over its body so thickly that they look like fur, as many as 300 feathers to a square inch! Only its leathery webbed feet, most of its bill, and its eyes are not covered with feathers.

The penguin's flippers, which are as hard as boards and do not fold as do ordinary bird's wings, are covered with small feathers. These feathers lie flat, overlapping each other like scales—white feathers on the inside, dark feathers on the outside. The feathers on the front edge are so short that you would need a magnifying glass to see that they are feathers and not scales.

Many scientists today believe the first penguins lived in warm southern seas, and that later some kinds moved down to Antarctica, the "world's ice box." Other scientists follow the beliefs of Alfred Lothair Wegener, who thought all the land in the world was once one great mass which gradually broke apart. Wegener believed that the curve of eastern South America fitted into that of the west coast of Africa, and Antarctica fitted with south Asia and Australia into the great land mass on the east coast of Africa. If this theory is correct, all penguins developed originally in warm seas. Then the

Emperor, Adélie, Chinstrap, and Gentoo Penguins drifted through many centuries with the Antarctic Continent until it came to anchor over the South Pole.

The 15 species of penguins are divided into six groups, or *genera,* which scientists have given Greek names. The first genus, Aptenodytes, means "wingless-divers." It includes two large antarctic penguins, the 38-inch King Penguin and the 48-inch Emperor Penguin. In all species of penguins the males are a little larger than the females. King and Emperor penguins hold their single egg on their feet while incubating it!

The second genus, Pygoscelis, means "rumplegged" and contains three species—the Gentoo, Adélie, and Chinstrap Penguins. The Greek name refers to the way these penguins' legs grow far back on their bodies, close to their stubby tails. These 30-inch antarctic birds nest on the ground, gathering pebbles, grasses, or whatever they can find to mark the spot where each female will lay two eggs.

The third genus, Eudyptes, meaning "good-diver," also contains three species—the 28-inch Crested, the 24-inch Rock-hopper, and the 28-inch Royal Penguin. These penguins all spend a whole season at sea. They live north of the Antarctic Circle, and

Admiral Richard Byrd, one of America's most famous explorers, brought back live Emperor Penguins to the United States in 1935.

lay their two eggs among the rocks on bare or pebble-strewn ground or in tussock grass.

The fourth genus, Megadyptes, meaning "mighty-diver," consists of a single species—the 30-inch Yellow-eyed Penguin. These birds breed only in southeastern New Zealand and on nearby Aukland and Campbell Islands. The females each lay two eggs in nests scattered in thick, bushy vegetation and heavy forest at the edge of the sea. Yellow-eyed Penguins stay in neighboring Pacific waters all year.

The fifth genus, Eudyptula, meaning "good-little-diver," contains the two smallest species—the 16-inch Blue and the slightly larger White-flippered Penguins. They live along the colder coasts of Australia and New Zealand and the small islets near them. These birds build nests of sticks, leaves, seaweed, and grass. The nests are placed in burrows they dig for themselves, or in caves or between rocks. Each pair raises two chicks a year.

The sixth genus is Spheniscus, from the Greek word for "small-wedge." This refers to the shape of the flippers of the four species that live the farthest away from the South Pole—the Jackass, Humboldt, Magellan, and Galapagos Penguins. The first three of these "wedge-flippers" nest in burrows they dig themselves, but the Galapagos Penguin has adapted to life on a volcanic island where digging is impossible. It nests on hard lava flows, in caves, or between or under rocks. Each of these four species raises two chicks each breeding season.

The history of this family of feathered, flippered fish-eaters is closely linked with the history of the great explorers who traveled south of the equator. Wherever these men went in their frail, wooden sailing ships, the penguins met them—just as they do today's explorers in their jets and helicopters.

11

EXPLORERS and PENGUINS

Explorers in the 16th and 17th centuries knew of the penguins in the southern oceans and wrote about them in their diaries. They did not describe them as a scientist would, however. Nor did they tell about them as tourists tell of interesting things they've seen on a holiday trip. The explorers wrote about penguins so the next adventurers would know a good source of food—much as we would tell a friend of a good restaurant we have found.

Canned goods and refrigerators had not yet been invented. All the food a ship carried was either dried, pickled, or salted. From Europe it took four to six months to reach the tip of South America if the winds were fair. When it got there, its supplies were exhausted.

In 1520, the Portuguese explorer Ferdinand Magellan discovered the straits named for him and the group of islands beyond it at the southern tip of South America. A man who kept a diary of Magellan's voyage wrote that as the ships followed the coast toward the "Pole Antarctic," they came to two islands so covered with penguins that in one hour all five ships could have been filled with them. He said, "The penguins live on fish and are so fat that they can scarcely be slayed. They have no feathers but a sort of down and their bills are like ravens' bills."

It is not a very good description. However, the month was October, when Magellan's Penguins breed on these islands, so we know they were the penguins Magellan saw. All penguins that live in cold climates have a thick layer of fat under their skin. It helps them to go without food when pack ice keeps them from the sea.

Thomas Cavendish, who sailed with the English admiral Sir Francis Drake, wrote in 1587 of another island in the Straits of Magellan: "We found a great store of fowl which could not fly, of the bigness of geese, whereof we killed in less than a day 3,000, and supplied ourselves well therewith."

Oliver Noort, a Dutch explorer, replenished his supplies with 50,000 penguins in 1599. It is a great wonder that there were any South American penguins left for the travelers of the next centuries.

None of the explorers of the 16th, 17th, and early 18th centuries showed much interest in animal or plant life unless they could eat it or use it for clothing. The Spanish brought home tomatoes, chocolate, potatoes, vanilla, sweet peppers, maize, nasturtiums, pumpkins, squash, and turkeys from South and Central America—along with a few live Indians. Sir Walter Raleigh carried tobacco home to England from North America, and John Rolfe brought his bride, Pocahontas. Not until the 18th century did an explorer take a naturalist with him to collect specimens of native plants and animals unknown to Europeans.

In 1768 Captain James Cook left England on the first of three voyages whose only aims were to bring back information about peoples, animals, plants, minerals, and the stars. While Captain Cook discovered new lands and peoples, his artists drew them and his scientists collected specimens. Among these collections were six species of penguins—the

An artist made this drawing of a King Penguin during Captain Cook's second voyage in 1775.

King Penguin, the Gentoo Penguin, the Chinstrap Penguin, the Rock-hopper Penguin, the Blue Penguin, and Magellan's Penguin. Their descriptions were published between 1778 and 1784. With the Jackass Penguin of Africa, seven penguins were known to science before 1800.

More than 30 years passed before another penguin

A modern photograph of a King Penguin.

was discovered. Explorers, taking naturalists with them, found the other eight species as they looked for the fabled continent of Antarctica, and later as they gradually visited every unexplored island in the world.

Among the penguins Captain Cook's ships brought home to England, the King Penguin was the first to be described and pictured. Naturalist John Reinhold Forster, who collected the bird on South Georgia Island, wrote of it in his diary, "This penguin has a peculiar noble and magnificent appearance, having an easy gait, a long neck when singing or crying, a longer and more elegant bill than other sorts, the back of more bluish cast, the belly more dazzling white, and a kind of necklace of bright yellow, which comes down on both sides of the head, as a boundary between the blue and the white and joins the belly."

But it was not until the 1950's, when scientists went to live in penguin colonies, that naturalists learned the details of King Penguin life.

King Penguins prepare themselves for courtship and mating with great care. After feeding and fattening at sea, they come ashore and stand around for four or five weeks while they *molt*. This means that their old feathers drop out and new ones grow in. During this time the birds doze with eyes half-closed, and they do not eat. They become so thin that the females weigh just 20 pounds. They probably lose one-third to one-half their weight. Then they go back to sea for another few weeks of feeding. This time when they come ashore they are plump and active. The male weighs up to 47 pounds, the

During molting, a bird loses its old feathers and grows new ones. The penguin at the right is molting.

female a little less, and they both look as though they are wearing wedding finery.

King Penguins do their courting at their breeding grounds on islands just north of the Antarctic Circle. The birds select low ground back from the sea, with a pool of flowing fresh water nearby. Here they gather in colonies of as many as 5,000. Each mated pair has its own bit of territory in the colony.

A pair of King Penguins may start courting any

time during the antarctic summer, which lasts from November to February. A male and female that are attracted to each other stand face to face. One bird bows gracefully, its bill touching its toes. Then it stretches its neck, pointing its bill toward the sky, and sends a musical bugle call echoing into the frosty air. If the second bird accepts the first, it returns the bow and bugle call.

The mated pair frolic about, stroll together, and go to sea to feed. They defend their own little territory from other house-hunting King Penguins. At the end of about a month the female lays one large egg. It is about 4½ inches long and 3 inches wide. The male bird, using its bill, gently lifts the egg on top of his own feet, tucks his tail against the back of it, and stands slightly stooped so a flap of loose skin on his belly falls over the front of the egg. He holds the egg this way, occasionally shuffling about a bit, but never letting it roll onto the cold, wet or snowy ground.

If an incubating King Penguin shuffles the two or three feet that bring it into a neighbor's territory, a fight takes place. Two birds carefully balancing eggs on their feet whack at each other, flippers flying and bills nipping. When such a fight starts the whole colony may become involved.

↑ *A pair of King Penguins with their egg.*

↓ *To incubate their eggs, these penguins hold them on their feet. A loose flap of skin on the stomach covers the egg and keeps it warm.*

While the male incubates, the female goes off to sea to fish. After 12 to 15 days the female comes back and the male transfers the egg to her feet and goes off to fish. Taking turns, the pair incubate the egg for 54 or 55 days. During the last few weeks they change places every four or five days.

When the downy chick first hatches, its parents hold it on their feet, tucked between flap and tail as the egg was held. It is fed on half-digested krill, squid, and fish, which the parents bring up from their stomachs and dribble into the open mouth of the chick. When the chick is fully feathered with down and too big to fit into its cradle, it starts to run about and joins a group of chicks. The parents feed the chick for 11 months, until it is ready to go to sea and feed itself. The chicks whistle when they are hungry, which is nearly all the time. Whistling chicks and bugling adults make a noisy colony.

It takes a pair of King Penguins 14 to 16 months to raise a single chick. A chick can only survive if its first trip to the sea is in the middle of the antarctic summer, between the first of December and early February. King Penguins take a new mate at each nesting and raise, one at a time, two young birds during a period of three years.

23

An adult King with its half-grown chick.

The
EMPEROR
PENGUIN

The largest member of the penguin family is the Emperor Penguin. Emperors and Kings are very much alike in appearance and habits, but an Emperor Penguin at its plumpest weighs a little over twice as much as a King at its plumpest. It is 10 inches taller. Emperors breed within or at the edge of the Antarctic Circle and Kings breed just north of it in the subantarctic.

To meet Emperor Penguins an explorer must enter Antarctica's continental waters. This, Sir James Ross did with the stout wooden ships, HMS "Erebus" and HMS "Terror," between 1839 and 1843.

25

He was on a British naval expedition, and his naturalists were his ships' doctors. They collected the first Emperor Penguins, 12 of them, from the floating ice during the antarctic summer and brought their skins back to England.

Thus, the world learned that near the Antarctic Continent, large penguins, larger than King Penguins, fished in the shadows of icebergs and took walks on blocks of floating ice. At the British Museum of Natural History, Mr. G. R. Gray officially described and named the Emperor Penguin from the 12 skins in 1844. The museum mounted two adults and one nearly grown chick in natural positions and put them in a glass case for people to see.

The world learned nothing more about the Emperor Penguin for 60 years. Between 1902 and 1904, Robert Falcon Scott led an expedition which spent two years in Antarctica, living on the ship "Discovery," frozen into the ice near land. The expedition made exploring trips on foot, pulling sledges with tents and supplies. On one of these trips along the coast in late July, two men found a colony of 2,000 breeding Emperor Penguins.

An elated naturalist, Dr. Edward Wilson, reported the news when he returned to England. He said that the Emperors held their small chicks on top

An artist's drawing of Robert Scott's ship, "Discovery."

of their feet, with a flap of feathered skin covering the chick in front and the tail protecting it behind. He wrote that the adult Emperor Penguins had such a great urge to care for a chick that those with none of their own tried to steal one. Any chick left untended by a parent was "actually killed with kindness," the chickless adults fighting over it until they tore it to pieces.

In 1911, Wilson returned to Antarctica with Scott. He was determined to reach the Emperors early enough to see the egg laying if possible, and collect eggs for the British Museum. On June 22,

27

Dr. Wilson and two companions, Apsley Cherry-Garrard and Lt. Henry R. Bowers, left Scott's hut on Ross Island bound for the Emperor colony, 70 miles away. They pulled two sledges that together weighed 757 pounds up ice mountains and across slender ice bridges over great ice canyons hundreds of feet deep. The temperatures dropped from 15° to 75° below zero—not ideal for camping in a tent. Blizzards raged. When after three weeks they finally reached the colony, they saw what they had come to find—Emperor Penguin eggs. However, they had arrived too late for egg laying.

In the darkness of the antarctic winter, the three men collected a number of eggs. But before they could get them back to the tent to preserve in alcohol, all but three burst from the cold.

Cherry-Garrard returned to England and delivered the three Emperor Penguin eggs, the first ever known, to the British Museum of Natural History. To his astonishment the chief curator received them with no ceremony and no thanks, just as though they were three chicken eggs he had bought at a nearby grocery store!

The complete life history of the Emperor Penguin was not known until 1952, when Dr. Jean Rivolier, the medical officer to a French expedition, reported the results of a year's study of an Emperor colony. The climate of Antarctica had not changed since Dr. Wilson's time, but expedition equipment had. A generator for electricity, radios, prefabricated buildings anchored by steel cables, insulated clothing and sleeping bags, vitamin pills, penicillin and other miracle drugs, instant foods, weasel tractors, walkie-talkies, new navigation instruments, and dozens of other recent inventions made life less dangerous and more comfortable for the seven penguin-watchers in French Antarctica.

Emperor Penguins spend the summer months of January and February at sea, fishing, riding on ice rafts, diving, and swimming. Their lemon-yellow breasts and necks sparkle in the sunlight that shines on them 24 hours a day. This is their migration time and they sometimes wander as far as 500 miles northward into subantarctic seas.

In early March, when the sun is still out during the day, the Emperors start homeward. By the end of March, the first breeding birds arrive at the same breeding grounds used in past years. From year to year a colony may move a few yards or a few miles to the spot where the ice is strongest, and icebergs and cliffs give greatest protection from storms.

A pair of courting Emperors.

In early April, when the sun rises for only a few hours to light the Emperor's icy world, the great "wingless-divers" start their courtship. Sometimes male woos female, sometimes female woos male. The wooer stands before the wooed, raising its head high. It rubs its head against one flipper, then the other, and then with head bowed very low it sings a musical trumpeting song. The song starts with low notes and works its way up to a long loud call. If the wooed one does not answer, the wooer moves on to woo another. But if the wooed one accepts the wooer, it bows its head and gives an inviting, cooing cackle. By the end of April, when the sun sinks for the four months of antarctic winter darkness, the center of the colony is packed with mated couples. Bachelor birds hang around outside the gathering.

In early May the first eggs appear. After a male fertilizes a female, it takes 25 days for the egg to form. The female lays it on the ice and immediately picks it up on her feet. The couple trumpet a duet for a few hours over the egg. Then the female lets it roll onto the ice and the male picks it up. Within 24 hours she leaves for the open sea to feed. The male holds the egg on his feet for 60 to 64 days, never letting it roll off. With other males, he stands patiently looking into the distance and dozing. When it storms the males stand together, shoulder to shoulder, with backs against the wind. They look like an enormous football team in a huddle.

Females usually return from the sea, fat and strong, just before the egg hatches in early August. They take over the last days of incubation while their starving mates go to sea. But sometimes the female is late and the male holds the downy chick when it hatches. When this happens, the male dribbles food formed by the flaking off of the lining of his empty stomach into the chick's mouth. As soon as the female appears she feeds the chick half-digested fish and shrimp.

By the 23rd of August the chicks begin to leave their parents' feet to run on their own. Soon they gather in groups called *creches*. Now both parents

Young Emperor Penguins gather in groups called creches.

go back and forth to the sea for food, leaving the chicks to take care of themselves. During good weather the parents are only with the chicks when feeding them. But when it storms, they may form a circle around their young, a living wall to protect them from the snow and wind.

In early November it is spring and the sun is shining again in Antarctica. The chicks are plump and strong and start to shed their baby down. Their new feathers are similar to the adult plumage, but with white instead of yellow at the throat and head. They are slightly smaller than their parents. At the end of November all the adults gather at the colony for their annual molt.

By Christmas day the Emperor Penguins start to wend their day back to the sea. They march in rows following a leader, and leap into the sea to fish before leaving on their migration.

In 1962 the Emperor Penguin population was estimated at 240,000 birds in 21 colonies. Emperor Penguins do not mature for a number of years. No one knows how old they are when they first mate and breed. One naturalist says probably five years old or older. Emperors are thought to live to be 50 to 75 years old.

CAPTAIN NAT PALMER and the RUMPLEGS

The best known of the penguins that breed on the Antarctic Continent is the charmer of the family, the curious Adélie, named for the wife of a French explorer. Adélie colonies are scattered all along the coasts of the continent. Several are on the long peninsula that points in the general direction of South America. Chinstrap and Gentoo Penguins are also found in these peninsula colonies. This is the only place in Antarctica where one can see all three "rumplegged" penguins leaping in and out of the sea on their way between their feeding grounds and their breeding grounds.

35

Stonington, Connecticut was famous for its fleet of ships that hunted seals in antarctic waters between 1820 and 1835. The seals were killed on their island breeding grounds. These animals were valuable for their fat, which was burned in lamps, and the seal skins, which were made into coats.

Nathaniel Brown Palmer was born in Stonington on August 8, 1799. When he was 13 years old he left his father's shipyard and went to sea. In 1820, a week before his 21st birthday, he became captain of the sloop "Hero." He sailed her with the Stonington fleet to the sealing grounds in the South Shetland Islands. When the fleet put into the harbor, they found very few seals ashore. So the commodore of the fleet sent young Captain Nat Palmer to explore southward for seal islands.

The sloop "Hero" was not much bigger than a lifeboat, but according to the ship's logbook, Captain Nat and his four-man crew sailed her as far as 63° 45' South. They stopped just off the Antarctic Peninsula. They found no fur seals, but they found what Captain Nat called "The Land" and on it on November 18, 1820, just as there have been every November since, were rumplegged penguins courting, nest building, and laying eggs in the antarctic spring.

Captain Nat and his crew were neither explorers nor naturalists, and they didn't think much of new land if it had no breeding seals on it. So they made no particular mention of what they had seen and done on their November sail until many years later. In a notebook Captain Nat wrote that they saw birds on "The Land," so we know they were the first men to see Adélie, Gentoo, and Chinstrap Penguins on the Antarctic Continent.

Captain Nat saw penguins with black heads, black throats, and black bills that looked at him with reddish eyes under white eyelids. These penguins walked on black-soled, brown-clawed, pink feet. They were Adélie Penguins. He saw penguins whose dark heads were crowned with a band of white feathers between and over their brown eyes. They had orange and black bills that matched their black-clawed, orange feet. These were the Gentoo Penguins. He also saw black-headed, black-billed penguins with pale tan eyes. They wore a black band across their white throats, like the hat strap under the chin of a guard at Buckingham Palace. They walked on pink-soled, gray-clawed, pink feet. These were the Chinstrap Penguins.

The Antarctic Peninsula is the only place where these rumplegs breed in mixed colonies—a group

It is easy to tell rumpleg penguins apart if you look at their faces. Above are the Adélie (left) and Chinstrap Penguin. Below is the Gentoo.

of mated Chinstraps in the middle of a Gentoo colony, or a group of mated Gentoos in an Adélie colony. One species may nest only a flipper length away from the other, yet the three do not mingle socially. Nor do they fight each other. All three fear the skuas, gull-like birds who feed their young on unprotected penguin eggs and weak penguin chicks. The three species of rumplegs have much in common, but their personalities are different.

The Chinstrap is inclined to fight. It seems to want to pick a quarrel with all its Chinstrap neighbors. The only time a group of Chinstraps agree is when a naturalist walks between their nests. Then they gang up to whack his legs black and blue with their flippers. A Chinstrap defends its nest, eggs, and young bravely. It prefers high parts of a colony and is a mountain climber, using beak, flippers, and feet to scramble up steep banks.

The Gentoo is the gentlest, most timid of the rumplegs. When disturbed, it makes a lot of noise and puts on a good bluff. But if the bluff doesn't work the Gentoo runs away. It does more pecking than flipper fighting. Gentoos flop down on their stomachs and toboggan over the snow more often than other rumplegs. They use their flippers as oars. Sometimes they coast down a slope and climb back up to repeat the trip. They appear to be having fun.

The Adélie Penguin is the most graceful of the rumplegs. Its walk is upright and smooth. When three or four move forward together, their flippers waving, they actually look like ballet dancers. A male Adélie attacks to protect his young, bumping the enemy with his breast, beating with his flippers, and biting with his bill. All through the attack he makes a noise that sounds like the rattle of a stick drawn along a picket fence. A female Adélie will defend her young if she has just returned from the sea and is well fed. But after a long fast, she will sometimes run away from an enemy.

Adélies squabble with their neighbors, usually with penguins of their own sex. When an Adélie walks among its neighbors' nests, it holds its flippers back close to its body, as if it were making an effort to be thin and not touch other penguins or their property.

Rumpleg penguins like to nest on rock-strewn ground. There is very little of this in icy Antarctica. Only in the most exposed places do the winds sweep the land clear of snow. So it is on the most unprotected beaches and mountain slopes that rumpleg colonies are found. On bare land in a

40

climate where no tree, shrub, or blade of grass can grow, these penguins raise their chicks—some near the sea, some a mile or more inland. A colony can be huge. More than a half-million Adélies nest flipper to flipper at Cape Crozier on the Ross Sea. In other colonies only a few hundred birds breed. Penguins usually return to the colony where they were hatched, but should it become overcrowded, younger birds are forced to go elsewhere.

Gentoo, Adélie, and Chinstrap Penguins all spend the winter months from March to October at sea. They dive off the pack ice to feed in open water. Young birds, who will not breed until they are about three or four years old, stay at sea the year round. Spring comes slowly in Antarctica and the

Many rumplegs build their nests of pebbles on the bare ground. This is a colony of nesting Adélies.

A pair of Adélies greet each other with a display.

rumplegs sometimes must walk over more than 100 miles of hard-frozen, rough sea ice to reach land.

The first birds reach shore in early October. They are the older, experienced adult males who have mated and raised young before. Each of them makes a beeline for his old nesting site, a few square feet of land he won and used in past years. He at once starts to collect small rocks and build a nest with them. A few days later his mate arrives and he greets her with what is called a *display*. He returns her bow, then stretches himself skyward,

42

A male steals a stone from another nest while his mate looks on.

pointing his bill to the heavens. He puffs out his chest, rolls his eyes, beats his flippers, and crows through his closed bill. His *ku-ku-ku-ku-ku* grows louder and louder and becomes *kug-gu-gu-gu-gu-ga-aaaa*. He ends his love call with soft growling notes, while touching his bill to first one of his shoulders and then the other.

Males without a mate do the display to attract one, and later over their eggs or young. A female who accepts a male returns his display and the pair face each other, swaying from side to side with bills pointing skyward. Then, while his mate takes over the nest building, the male goes in search of more stones. Sometimes he goes out of the colony to find one, but often he steals from a neighbor, nipping a stone out of a nest when the neighbor's back is turned. Displaying and stealing stones are continued off and on during the entire breeding season until the fledged chicks go off to sea. The worst thieves have the biggest nests, a pile of stones with a hollow on the top to hold the eggs. Chicks with an honest father may hatch on the cold bare ground.

A female rumpleg penguin usually lays two eggs. They are greenish-white, a little longer than they are wide, and a little smaller than tennis balls. A female lays her second egg three days after the first. She may lay them as early as the first week in November or as late as mid-December.

Adélie Penguins go without food from the time they come ashore until the eggs are laid. Then the female returns to sea to feed, and the male fasts for two more weeks while he incubates the eggs. When the female comes home, fat and saucy, the hungry male takes his two weeks at sea. He takes over the last incubation duty while his mate feeds again. She comes back ready to feed predigested krill to the chicks when, after 35 to 37 days,

44

A hungry skua tries to steal a penguin egg. This unusual photograph was taken during Robert Scott's last Antarctic expedition of 1910-1912.

they chip their way out of the eggs. By the first of January, the chicks can be left alone. It is mid-summer and the shore ice is gone, so the adults can go back and forth to the water to feed themselves and their chicks without traveling such long distances.

The Chinstrap and Gentoo Penguins do not lay their eggs until the first of December. The mated

45

A proud-looking parent and its chick.

pairs take turns at the nest in shorter periods, each
fishing daily through the 35 to 37 days of incubation. Sometimes a parent bird incubates for only
an hour or two, sometimes for as long as 30 hours.
Gentoo and Chinstrap chicks start hatching the
second week in January.

For the first few weeks after they hatch, rumpleg
chicks are brooded by the parents. The parents
cover them and keep them warm just as a hen does
her chicks. They grow very fast and by the time

46

they are two or three weeks old they start to leave the nest. They gather together in large creches. The parents continue to feed the chicks, calling them out of the creche. Each chick recognizes the voices of its own parents. Adults will feed only their own young. Orphaned or deserted chicks are ignored and starve to death.

When they are eight weeks old, rumpleg chicks are the same size as their parents. They have lost their baby down and grown the feathers they will wear for a year. The adults stop feeding them and feed themselves to fatten for their yearly molt. Molting

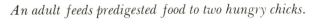

An adult feeds predigested food to two hungry chicks.

penguins do not go swimming, so they cannot fish or feed. The adult Adélies leave their young at the nesting grounds. They molt a few weeks later, standing around on the floating pack ice. Chinstraps and Gentoos molt standing near their nests. The young go off to sea by themselves. Without being led they know where to go, and without being taught they know how to swim and fish and what to eat.

Adélie Penguins leap into the sea headfirst from ice cliffs. When they leave the water, they are often faced with a cliff six feet high. As though jumping from a trampoline they shoot up to the ice with no effort at all. Gentoos and Chinstraps are more apt to waddle in and out of the water at a shallow beach.

Gentoo Penguins also nest on such islands as the Falklands, off the tip of South America. In Antarctica the temperature clings to the freezing point, but in the Falklands it rises well above that to 47° Fahrenheit in mid-summer. Tussock grass and red crowberry, called "diddle dee" by the Falkland Islanders, grow on the Gentoos' nesting grounds. The birds use twigs of the diddle dee to build their nests. Instead of stealing stones from one another, the males steal diddle-dee twigs.

49

Scientists are trying to find out more about how penguins live. This man is studying a group of Adélies.

The PENGUIN CLOWNS

Those crested penguins known as the "good-divers" are the natural clowns of the penguin family. Their progress on land has neither grace nor dignity. When they walk they lift their feet high, lean forward, and lurch unsteadily from side to side. When in a hurry they jump with both feet. Looking at a group of them moving along the beach is like watching a sack race. As they land, they wobble as though about to fall flat on their faces, then recover their balance, straighten up, and leap again. The tufts of yellow feathers on their heads shake like pompons on a skating cap, and they bray like donkeys as they bounce along.

51

The Rock-hopper Penguin, one of the clowns of the family.

The smallest of the three clowning good-divers is the two-foot-high Rock-hopper Penguin. Captain James Cook's sailors called it the "Jumping-jack," a name that truly describes the Rock-hopper ashore. It is red-eyed and red-billed, and does its jumping on black-soled, brown-clawed, pink feet.

The second clowning good-diver is usually called the Royal Penguin. As there is nothing royal about its behavior, this English name must be in honor of some royal person. It is also often called the Macaroni Penguin, but not in honor of Italian macaroni. In the late 18th and early 19th centuries "macaroni" was a slang word for a dude or dandy —a ridiculously overdressed young man. It also could mean something a dude would wear, as in:

> "Yankee Doodle came to town,
> A-riding on a pony,
> He stuck a feather in his cap
> And call'd it macaroni."

The yellow feathers on the head of this bird may be what give it the name Macaroni Penguin. It jumps on black-soled, pink feet, with gray webs between its toes and brown and white claws. The red tip on its brownish bill matches its eyes, over which hang long golden head plumes. The Royal

A pair of Royal or Macaroni Penguins out for a stroll.

Penguin also wears a band of yellow feathers across its forehead.

The last of the three clowning good-divers is the Crested Penguin. Its golden crests start just back of its reddish-brown bill, pass over its brown eyes, and point toward the back of its head. The crests are stiffer than those of the Rock-hopper and Royal Penguins. The Crested Penguin hops and jumps on

53

brown-soled, brown-clawed, brown-webbed, pinkish-white feet. Crested and Royal Penguins are four inches taller than Rock-hopper Penguins.

These three penguins have very heavy bills and use them as weapons. The man who dares to get in a penguin's way as it rock-hops will be attacked by an angry bird that leaps in the air to catch his sleeve. The penguin hangs on, swinging from its bill and slapping with its flippers. Getting rid of such a hanging penguin is no easy task. The males are much more aggressive than the females.

The "Antarctic convergence" is the place north of the Antarctic Continent where cold currents of water come to the surface of the oceans. The cold currents carry rich food up from the bottom of the sea—plankton, shrimp, octopus, and fish, upon which penguins feed. The good-divers breed on islands near the Antarctic convergence and north-ward to the Falkland Islands, to Tristan da Cunha, and to New Zealand. In winter they travel up the east coast of South America as far as Buenos Aires in Argentina and to Tasmania and Australia. They don't go to the coasts of Antarctica at all.

The good-divers spend at least half the year at sea. Breeding birds return each year as long as they live to the same mate and the same nesting site.

They come ashore in October and, like other penguins, fast during the period of courtship and nest building. They use anything they can find in building the nest. When they find grass, twigs, leaves, and moss, as the Crested Penguin does in New Zealand, they use them. Birds on a barren island may use stones, bones of penguins long dead, or bits of seaweed and driftwood washed up by the sea. Crested Penguins also nest in caves. If nothing but bare ground or rock is available, the females lay their two eggs directly on it.

Good-divers incubate their eggs standing upright. They lift the eggs onto their own feet, letting a flap of loose skin fall over them, as King and Emperor Penguins do. When they get tired of standing around holding the eggs, they drop them and flop down on their stomachs to cover them—the way an Adélie Penguin does.

The females incubate the eggs for the first few weeks while the males go to sea to fish. These penguins have no sea ice to travel over on foot. The ice-free ocean is only a few hundred feet from their colonies. But the birds may have a long swim. The schools of fish are often many miles away and do not move near the island coasts until the eggs start hatching in December.

A Royal Penguin breeding grounds on Macquarie Island.

For the first two or three weeks of a chick's life, its father stands guard over it day and night. He broods it on his feet for the first few days, and after that covers it on the nest. The female goes back and forth to the sea, bringing food to the chick. While she is feeding it, the male stands guard. When the chick leaves the nest of its own accord and joins a creche, both parents go to sea. By this time the male has fasted 21 to 30 days.

For these penguins having the male in charge is a very good arrangement. The male bravely fights off enemies, while the more timid female is apt to run away. The chick is more likely to survive guarded by a brave male. The enemies of good-diver chicks are troublesome bachelor birds that try to steal nests and nest sites. Chicks so driven from their own nests will be flipper-slapped and possibly pecked to death by neighboring adults. They may also become the prey of hungry skuas.

A colony of Rock-hopper, Royal, or Crested Penguins may have many thousands of pairs occupying many acres. One Royal Penguin colony on Macquarie Island covers 16½ acres of the island. Or a colony may be as small as a few hundred pairs. The birds go back and forth between the colony and the water along pathways made by their own

58

feet. All those going to the sea use one path and all leaving the sea use another. If they enter the water from a cliff they jump feet first, instead of swan diving as do the Adélie penguins.

A Rock-hopper, Royal, or Crested Penguin colony is not a pleasant place to visit. An individual good-diver has a goatlike smell. Hundreds of penguins together plus the horrid smell of half-digested fish that missed the chick's open bill, gives the colony an overpowering odor.

In February, full-grown chicks leave the colonies and go to sea. Shortly afterward their parents also head for the sea for a month of fattening. Then they return to the colony to molt. It takes about 17 days for the birds to lose their old feathers and another 14 days for their new ones to grow in. When the good-divers return to the sea in April, it is to dive and swim until the following October. Little is known of their movements during these winter months except that they go northward. Undoubtedly they follow the cold currents of water laden with plankton, fish, and krill.

Good-diver penguins may be clowns on land and when entering the water, but they are truly at home in the ocean. They swim through the water without effort, and leap to the surface with a grace

Good-diver penguins take to the water with ease.

entirely lacking in their leaps on shore. Many stay at sea long enough to grow barnacles on their feet.

The voyages of Captain James Cook brought back to England the Rock-hopper Penguin, which was described and named in 1784. His naturalists also collected a Crested Penguin, but it lay forgotten and unnoticed in the British Museum. Not until 1843 was the Crested Penguin named and described by Mr. G. R. Gray.

The voyages that brought the Royal Penguin back to Europe are of great interest to historians. They were Russian voyages, and Soviet Russia's claims to land in Antarctica are based on them. In

1819, Czar Alexander I sent out an exploring expedition under the command of Baron Fabian Gottlieb Von Bellingshausen. Baron Von Bellingshausen had scientists with him but no naturalists. Nevertheless he collected natural history specimens, as he had been directed to do.

At the Falkland Islands the Russians found the Royal Penguin. It was named and described in 1837 by a German, Dr. Johann F. Brandt, at the Russian Imperial Academy of Science. In those days Russia had hardly any scientists of its own. Almost all the scientists, doctors, and teachers were Germans brought to Russia by the Czar to raise Russia's standards of learning.

When Baron Von Bellingshausen returned to Russia in 1821 the Czar did not want to spend any money to publish the expedition's discoveries. But the fear that the world would not recognize Russia's claims in Antarctica made him change his mind in 1831. In recent years the Soviet Union has published many old diaries and letters of the expedition to back up their claims in Antarctica. Soviet scientists now on the Antarctic Continent are adding to what we know about penguins. The Russian name for the penguin they discovered means "the Golden-haired Penguin" in English.

PECULIAR PENGUINS

The coasts of southern Australia and northern New Zealand are home to the smallest species of penguin, one of the two "good-little-divers." The Australians call it the Little or Fairy Penguin. Visitors vacationing at Philip Island near Melbourne gather each night to see what is known as "The Penguin Parade." From 500 to 700 Fairy Penguins who have been out fishing come ashore and follow each other up the beach toward their nesting ground. They march in groups or platoons, each with a leader. The birds have become a famous attraction at the summer resort island and a huge spotlight illuminates their landing place.

63

"The Penguin Parade" on Philip Island.

A group of Fairy Penguins approaches the shore with noisy chattering barks. They hesitate at the edge of the water. The leader barks a signal and off the group waddles, making way for the next platoon. None of the birds pays any attention to the watching people or the glaring spotlight. Each is intent on spending a few hours with its mate in the nesting burrow. Before daylight the fishermen usually take over the nesting duties with eggs or chicks, and their hungry mates go to sea to feed until parade time the next night.

In New Zealand, Fairy Penguins are called Blue Penguins. The feathers on the backs and heads of these small birds are blue with black shafts. Their flippers are dark except for two rows of white feathers on the back edges. Little, Blue, or Fairy Penguins parade on black-clawed, brown-soled, pinkish-white feet. Silver-blue eyes shine above their brown and black bills.

Very much like the Fairy Penguin is the second good-little-diver, the White-flippered Penguin. Both edges of its flippers are white, its back and head are more gray than blue, and it is 16½ inches high—a half-inch taller than the Fairy Penguin. It breeds only on one small bit of the New Zealand coast, the Banks Peninsula.

64

One other penguin lives in New Zealand. It is the Yellow-eyed Penguin, the only species in the genus called "mighty-diver." Black and yellow feathers cover the upper part of its face. A circle of golden feathers on its head looks like a crown, and matches its golden eyes above a russet and white bill. This penguin goes about on brown-clawed, brown-soled, pink feet.

The Fairy Penguin, the White-flippered Penguin, and the Yellow-eyed Penguin never see ice or snow. They do not migrate, but remain near their breeding places the year round. Although south Australia is bleak and chilly, and New Zealand coasts are cool in winter, in summer the temperatures go as high as 85° F. These birds have adapted, or changed, to get along in warm climates. Their feathers are shorter than those of their antarctic relatives. Bare patches of skin near their bills allow heat to escape from their bodies. They stay at sea during the day and come ashore in the cool of the night. Here they nest in burrows or caves, under tree roots in forests, or under rocks. During the time they are incubating their two eggs and caring for their chicks, they stay under cover while the sun is up. At night they become active, bringing their chicks out of the burrows for fresh air.

Fairy Penguins are the smallest members of the penguin family.

Fairy and White-flippered Penguins are nocturnal birds and, like owls, have big eyes designed to see at night. Owls and many other birds must move their necks to see on either side. But all penguins see to the side by moving the pupils of their eyes, as do human beings.

The Fairy, White-flippered, and Yellow-eyed Penguins nest in loose colonies. Each mated pair is at least 10 yards from its nearest neighbor. Very little fighting goes on between the birds. These distant neighbors only meet on pathways that lead to the sea and at the landing places. There they bark and bow to one another.

Courtship starts in late August with trumpeting, bowing, and posing, and then nest digging or building. To caress one another, the mated pair stand either breast to breast, or with the male behind the female. The male puts his flippers around his mate and beats a tattoo on her. Both male and female nibble each other's neck feathers.

Between caresses each bird dips its bill into the oil in its preen gland, just above its tail, and dresses its own and its mate's feathers. All penguins preen, dress, and smooth their plumage, but birds in warm climates do so more often. After preening, the pair may yawn. Then they close their eyes and sleep either standing up or lying on their stomachs.

The Yellow-eyed Penguin may nest in a burrow or under tussock grass or ferns. When it is not in

A Yellow-eyed Penguin in its nest of grass and sticks beneath a hollow tree.

a burrow it builds a nest of sticks and grass two to three feet in diameter. In the burrows, all three species may put down a little grass for a nest, or be quite content with bare ground.

The females each lay two eggs, the second two or three days after the first, in September or October. The eggs are incubated for about six weeks. Often only one egg hatches and the other is pushed out of the nest. The chicks hatch helpless and blind. Yellow-eyed chicks are guarded by one parent or the other for the first six weeks of their lives, the Fairy and White-flippered chicks for the first four weeks. The parent not on guard goes off to fish and brings predigested food home to the chicks. Yellow-eyed Penguins feed their chicks by dribbling the fish into their open bills. Fairy and White-flippered chicks put their heads into the gaping mouth of a stooping parent and help themselves.

When they are old enough not to be guarded, good-little-diver chicks stay close to the nesting site. Yellow-eyed chicks wander about, sometimes alone, sometimes with three or four other chicks, but never in a creche.

Fairy, White-flippered, and Yellow-eyed Penguins all come ashore often at night the year around,

Two half-grown Yellow-eyed chicks.

some near their nesting places. Others come ashore wherever they happen to land after following the schools of krill, yellow-eyed mullet, red cod, and squid.

The Fairy Penguin was first brought back to Europe by the naturalists who traveled with our old friend, Captain James Cook. The White-flippered Penguin was described and named in 1874 by a German scientist, Dr. Otto Finsch, who had never seen New Zealand but had a collection of its birds. The Yellow-eyed Penguin was named and described by two French naturalists, Hombron and Jacquinot, who collected it in 1840 during an antarctic exploring expedition commanded by Dumont d'Urville.

69

PROBLEM PENGUINS

The four species of penguins that are known as the "wedge-flippers" are the Jackass Penguin of South Africa, and the Magellan, Humboldt, and Galapagos Penguins of South America. They are a problem to scientists because they look so much alike that some naturalists believe they are not four species at all, but one species that lives in four separate places. All four are white-fronted, brownish-black birds with a dark stripe across their chests, and a white stripe on either side of their heads. They walk on black legs and feet with whitish marks on the webbing between their toes.

Jackass   _Magellan_

Because they look so much alike,

They have reddish-brown eyes and dark bills.

The wedge-flippers are a problem to write about because although they live closer to civilization than any other penguins and are even kept as pets in South America, they have never been well-studied. Perhaps scientists feel it is more adventurous to go off to antarctic regions than it is to go to South America and South Africa, where penguins swim with the bathers on the beaches. Many naturalists from the United States have studied

Humboldt　　　　　　　　　　　　　　　*Galapagos*

some scientists think these four penguins may be just one species.

South American birds, but not one has stayed in a penguin rookery to watch marked birds throughout an entire breeding season.

The wedge-flippers bray like jackasses during the night on their nesting grounds. They bray and bow and do the display when courting just like other penguins. All wedge-flippers like to place their carelessly made nests under cover. Magellan, Humboldt, and Jackass Penguins nest in burrows they dig themselves—the Jackass on low sandy islands, the

73

others in forests under tree roots or in sandy slopes, where they tunnel as deep as eight feet into a bank. Humboldt and Galapagos Penguins often place their nests under overhanging rocks, or in caves. Because the Galapagos Penguin cannot dig into the hardened, rock-like lava of the volcanic islands, it sometimes has to nest on the open lava slopes. Here near the equator, 500 miles from the coast of Ecuador, these birds breed in May, June, and July. Humboldt Penguins nest during most of the year on the warm islands off Peru. Magellan Penguins breed in November, December, and January. Each pair raises two chicks.

Wedge-flippers waddle along on land and drop on their stomachs, using not only flippers but feet to push themselves over the sand. Ashore they sleep squatting or standing. In the water they turn on their sides to sleep with one foot in the air. Wedge-flippers cover their eggs and their chicks just like a sitting hen. It takes 39 days for Jackass chicks to hatch, but incubation times are unknown for the other three species.

The wedge-flippers are valuable to farmers, who use their droppings as fertilizer. This guano is used in both Africa and South America. The sale of penguin eggs brings an income to the government

74

Two Jackass Penguins peer out of a burrow they have dug in the ground.

of South Africa that owns and protects Dassen Island, the largest breeding colony of Jackass Penguins. Penguin eggs are considered as good to eat and cook with as chicken eggs.

Every year in late August a great number of penguins come ashore at Dassen Island and start digging their burrows. Their feet make little fountains of sand spurt into the air a few feet apart all over the two square miles of the island. When the tunnels are finished the female Jackass Penguins begin to lay eggs.

Every morning from September through November a crew of government employees goes out to collect penguin eggs. With a large kitchen spoon tied to a long stick, the men reach into the two- to three-foot nesting tunnels and scoop the eggs out from under the incubating birds. During the early part of this century 300,000 eggs a year were taken from the island and sold in the cities of South Africa. Even though female penguins do not lay extra eggs to replace stolen ones, plenty of eggs were left to hatch on Dassen Island. Each female Jackass Penguin lays two and sometimes three eggs, and more than four million pairs of penguins bred on the island during those years. The size of the Jackass Penguin population is unknown today, but eggs are still being collected and sold.

The Spanish and Portuguese explored and settled most of South America, but they never described or named a penguin. The Jackass and Magellan Penguins were named in England. Franz J. F. Meyen, a German doctor-naturalist on a round-the-world discovery cruise, collected and named the Humboldt Penguin in 1830. Dr. John Gustaf Hjalmar Kinberg, a Swedish doctor-naturalist making the first Swedish world exploration on the frigate "Louise," collected the Galapagos Penguin in 1851. It lay in the museum in Stockholm for 19 years before a Swedish scientist decided that it was a new penguin and described and named it.

Penguins were and still are lifesavers to marooned

and hungry explorers and scientists. In February, 1916, Sir Ernest Shackleton and his shipwrecked men were starving on the floating pack ice off the Antarctic Peninsula. They killed 600 birds during one week when they found Adélie Penguins traveling to the open sea. Adélie stews and steaks kept the men alive until more nourishing seals were met.

Centuries before European explorers discovered these penguins, native African tribes and South American Indians were eating them and their eggs and wearing their skins. Because the birds were unable to fly, they were easy to catch and kill with that most primitive weapon, a club. The only garment the Tierra del Fuegans wore when Magellan met them in 1520 was a short cape of Magellan Penguin skins on their shoulders. Their women were dressed in aprons made of a single penguin skin.

During the 18th century, penguin skins were used to make muffs, hats, table mats, and feather trimming, and men went to penguin colonies to collect penguin eggs, skins, and oil. Today scientists go there to study the penguins. They hope to learn more about how each species lives. And they believe that from the behavior of these sociable birds they may learn something that can be used in the study of human behavior.

Where Penguins Live
- Penguin nesting places

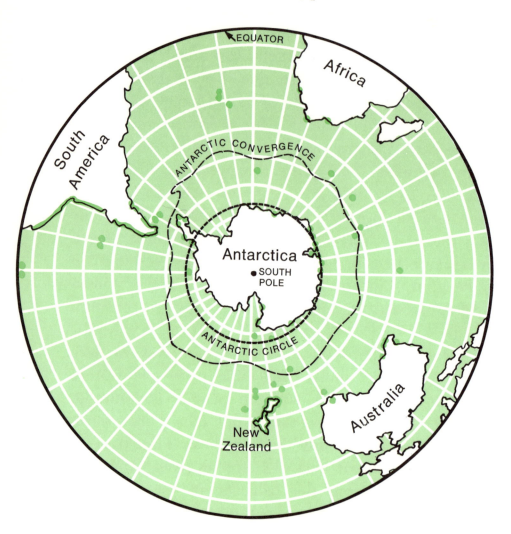

Author's Note

My husband, Oliver L. Austin, Jr., introduced me to penguins when he returned from Antarctica in 1956 with pictures of Adélie Penguins from five colonies on the shores of the Ross Sea. I continued to learn by reading the reports of scores of explorers and naturalists, among them those men mentioned in the text, and also particularly the studies of penguins made by Robert Cushman Murphy, Eleanor and Olin Sewall Pettingill, and Richard Penney of the U.S.A., Jean Prevost of France, T. W. Bagshawe of England, Robert A. Falla, F. C. Kinsky, and Launcelot Richdale of New Zealand, and Donald Serventy and John Warham of Australia.

I have profited most greatly from the researches of William J. L. Sladen of Johns Hopkins University and Antarctica, who has lived with and studied penguins for the past 20 years. Dr. Sladen took time from his heavy schedule to read my manuscript. I am most grateful to him for his knowledgeable critique. I am also most grateful to, and respect the abilities of Random House editor Jean Van Leeuwen, with whom it has been a pleasure to cooperate.

My husband's colleagues Pierce Brodkorb, Mary Heimerdinger Clench, and E. G. Franz Sauer were generous with time and information. Correspondence with G. J. Broekhuysen of Cape Town, South Africa and Averil Lysaght of London, England was most helpful. Without the wholehearted cooperation of the outstanding staff of the University of Florida Libraries, this book would never have been finished.

Index

About the Author

ELIZABETH S. AUSTIN is a Research Associate on the staff of the Florida State Museum where her husband, well-known ornithologist Oliver L. Austin Jr., is curator of ornithology. With her husband, Mrs. Austin is the author of *The Look-It-Up Book of Birds,* and has contributed the material on birds for the *Junior Encyclopedia of Natural History.*

For several years, Mrs. Austin wrote a weekly nature column for a Florida newspaper. She is the editor of a recent adult book, *Frank M. Chapman in Florida.* Dr. and Mrs. Austin live in Gainesville, Florida.